Table of Contents

Table of Contents

Gluten-Free Dump Dinners & Desserts

Warning: While we make every attempt to write our recipes for gluten-free ingredients, many ingredients can vary by manufacturer. You must be careful to read labels and warnings, and stay aware of changing regulations regarding labeling. The safest way to eat gluten-free is by using fresh ingredients. Second, look for the certified gluten-free label. Third, call the manufacturer yourself to ask if the product is gluten-free, and produced in a designated gluten-free facility. Even if gluten products are not listed in the ingredients, it is possible to pick up airborne flour, for example, in a facility that is not dedicated gluten-free. Wheat-free is not the same as gluten-free. For example, modified corn starch, barley, and oats may contain gluten. Products you may not think of containing gluten may in fact contain gluten. A few of these include: spices such as cinnamon and cumin; canned goods such as broth and soup; sauces and salad dressings. The bottom line is to be vigilant about checking labels, and consulting the manufacturer when in doubt.

Whether you or a loved one must avoid gluten for medical reasons, or you've realized how much better you feel living gluten-free, the recipes in this collection will soon become some of your best-loved dishes. You'll find that creating gluten-free meals, side dishes and desserts for family and friends doesn't need to be intimidating. In fact, the recipes in this book make cooking gluten-free as easy as 1-2-3—simply combine the ingredients, stir, and bake. These recipes are so satisfying and stress-free you'll never miss the gluten. You'll find many healthy alternatives to the comfort foods we crave, and along the way might just discover brand new family favorites.

EASY OVEN FAJITAS

Ingredients:
1 yellow onion, sliced thin
2 medium green bell peppers, sliced into thin strips
1 medium red bell pepper, sliced into thin strips
1 lb steak, cut into thin strips
1 package gluten-free fajita seasoning
2 Tbsp canola oil
1 medium lime (optional)
8 (6-inch) gluten-free flour tortillas
1/2 cup sour cream
Cheddar cheese, shredded
Salsa
Avocado slices

Directions:
Preheat the oven to 400°. Place the sliced onion, peppers, and meat into a 9 x 13 inch baking dish. Sprinkle the seasoning over the meat and vegetables. Drizzle the vegetable oil over all and then toss the ingredients until everything is well coated in oil and seasoning. Bake for 35-40 minutes, stirring once half way through. Squeeze the juice from half of the lime over top of the fajita mixture after it comes out of the oven. To serve, scoop a small amount of fajita mixture into the center of each tortilla. Top with sour cream, cheese, salsa, and avocado slices.

Note: Chicken can be substituted for the beef, if desired.

BEEF AND VEGETABLES IN A SKILLET

Ingredients:
1/2 tsp salt
4 medium zucchinis, cut into spirals (use a vegetable spiralizer or slice very thin)
2 Tbsp olive oil
3 cloves garlic, diced
1 lb beef, sliced thin (like for fajitas)
1 Tbsp onion, minced
1 cup fresh mushrooms, sliced
3 Tbsp tapioca flour
2 cups gluten-free beef stock
2 cups broccoli florets
Salt and pepper, to taste

Directions:
Place the thin sliced zucchini into a colander and toss with salt. Set aside for 20–30 minutes. Meanwhile, in a large skillet, combine the oil, garlic, beef, onion, and mushrooms. Sauté until vegetables are tender and then, add the tapioca flour, stirring to coat. Continue stirring while adding in the beef stock, broccoli, and zucchini. Cover and simmer until broccoli and zucchini are tender, but not overcooked, about 3-5 minutes.

OVEN BAKED GOULASH

Ingredients:
1 lb lean ground beef, browned
1 28-oz can stewed tomatoes
1 onion, chopped
2 stalks of celery, chopped
1 4-oz can of mushrooms, drained
1 14.5-oz can corn, drained
1 14.5-oz can tomato sauce
2 bay leaves
2 tsp oregano
2 cups (more or less) fresh mashed potatoes

Directions:
Preheat oven to 350°. Spray a 9 x 13 inch pan with non-stick cooking spray. Combine all ingredients in the prepared dish, stirring gently. Top with mashed potatoes. Bake for 20-30 minutes or until heated through and potatoes are lightly browned around the edges.

BEEF STROGANOFF

Ingredients:
1 lb lean ground beef or steak (cut into bite size pieces)
4 oz fresh mushrooms, sliced
1 Tbsp butter
2 Tbsp gluten-free all-purpose flour
1 cup gluten-free beef broth
1/2 cup sour cream
Salt and pepper to taste

Directions:
In a large skillet, cook beef until browned; drain any excess grease. Add mushrooms and butter, sautéing until soft. Mix in flour until everything is coated. Slowly pour in the broth and cook until slightly thickened. Stir in sour cream. Season with salt and pepper. Continue simmering on low until sauce is hot. Serve over gluten-free pasta or rice.

CORN CHIP PIE

Ingredients:
1 lb lean ground beef
1/2 cup onion, diced
1 15-oz can kidney beans, rinsed and drained
1 15-oz can corn, drained
1 10 3/4-oz can gluten-free condensed tomato soup
1 package gluten-free taco seasoning
1-2 cups water
Corn chips
2-4 cups cheddar cheese, shredded
Sour cream (optional)

Directions:
In a large cooking pot, combine the ground beef and onion, cooking until beef is browned and onion is tender. Drain grease off. Add the beans, corn, tomato soup, and seasoning. Stir together and then add water until desired consistency. Bring to a boil and cook for about 5 minutes. Put corn chips in the bottom of soup bowls. Ladle the ground beef mixture onto the corn chips and sprinkle shredded cheese over the top. Put a dollop of sour cream on top of the cheese, if desired.

CHILLY DAY CHILI

Ingredients:
1 lb extra-lean ground beef
1 onion, diced
1 pkg gluten-free chili seasoning
1 tsp cumin
1 Tbsp oregano
1 can stewed tomatoes
1 can tomato sauce
1 can kidney beans

Directions:
In a Dutch oven or large sauce pan, brown the ground beef. Add the onion to sauté while the meat is still cooking. Mix in the rest of the ingredients, stirring to combine. Cook on low-medium heat, until hot and bubbling. Reduce heat and simmer for at least an hour. Serve with shredded cheese, corn chips and a dollop of sour cream, if desired.

Main Dishes

SHEPHERD'S PIE

Ingredients:
1 1/2 lbs extra-lean ground beef
1/2 cup chopped onion
1/4 cup tomato paste
1 tsp Italian seasoning
Salt and pepper to taste
1 12-oz bag frozen green beans
1 24-oz package refrigerated garlic mashed potatoes
(or left-over potatoes)
1 cup cheddar cheese, shredded

Directions:
Heat oven to 350°. In a large skillet, cook beef and onion over medium-high heat 6 to 8 minutes, stirring occasionally, until thoroughly cooked; drain any excess grease. Stir in the tomato paste, Italian seasoning, salt and pepper. Spread the meat mixture evenly on the bottom of the skillet. Spread green beans over top of meat mixture. Spoon the potatoes evenly over the beans and meat. Spread cheese over all. Cover and bake 20 to 25 minutes or until cheese is melted and casserole is heated through.

ASIAN BEEF STIR-FRY

4 Tbsp olive oil
1 lb beef steak, thinly sliced (sirloin steak strips, flank steak, or any other steak)
1 1/2 cups fresh mushrooms, sliced thinly
2 cups snow peas
1 15.25-oz can white corn
1/2 cup low-sodium gluten-free soy sauce
1/3 cup brown sugar
6 garlic cloves, minced
1/2 tsp ginger
2 tsp rice vinegar
2 cups cooked rice

Directions:
Heat a large skillet until hot, add the olive oil. Add the meat, making sure that each slice browns nicely. Add mushrooms, stirring occasionally, until they brown nicely. Add the snow peas and corn, then the seasoning and rice vinegar. Stir everything to combine and let cook for about 1 minute. Turn off heat. Cover the skillet with a lid. Serve over rice.

OLD FASHIONED MEATBALLS AND MASHED POTATOES

Ingredients:
1 18-oz package gluten-free frozen meatballs
1 onion, diced
1 10.5-oz can gluten-free condensed French onion soup
2-4 cups prepared fresh mashed potatoes (left-over potatoes are perfect for this recipe)

Directions:
Preheat the oven to 375°. In an 8 x 8 inch baking dish, combine the meatballs and onions. Pour in the French onion soup. Spread the potatoes over the top. Cover the dish with aluminum foil. Bake for 20 minutes. Uncover and continue baking until potatoes are browned around the edges.

DELICIOUS TEX-MEX MASH-UP

Ingredients:
16 oz gluten-free wide egg noodles, cooked and drained
1 1/4 cups gluten-free enchilada sauce
1 15-oz can corn, drained
1 can black beans, drained and rinsed
1/4 cup plain Greek yogurt
1 4-oz can diced green chiles
1 lb ground beef, cooked and crumbled
4 oz cream cheese, softened
1/2 tsp chili powder, more or less to taste
1/4 tsp cumin
1 cup shredded cheddar cheese, divided
1 cup shredded Monterey Jack cheese, divided

Directions:
Preheat oven to 350°. Spray a 9 x 13 inch baking dish with non-stick cooking spray. In a large bowl, stir together all of the ingredients except 1/2 cup of each of the shredded cheeses. Pour into the prepared baking dish. Top with remaining cheeses. Place into oven and bake until heated through and cheese is melted, about 20-25 minutes. Serve with avocado slices, sour cream, and salsa.

SOUTHWESTERN STYLE CASSEROLE

Ingredients:

2 cups prepared gluten-free Spanish style rice
1 1/4 cups gluten-free enchilada sauce
1 can corn, drained
1 can black beans, drained and rinsed
1/4 cup plain Greek yogurt
1 4-oz can diced green chiles
1 lb ground beef, cooked and crumbled
4 oz cream cheese, softened
1/2 tsp chili powder, more or less to taste
1/4 tsp cumin
1 cup shredded cheddar cheese, divided
1 cup shredded Monterey Jack cheese, divided

Directions:

Preheat oven to 350 degrees. Spray a 9 x 13 inch baking dish with non-stick cooking spray. In a large bowl, stir together all of the ingredients except 1/2 cup of each of the shredded cheeses. Pour into the prepared baking dish. Top with remaining cheeses. Place into oven and bake until cheese is melted, about 20-25 minutes. Serve with avocado slices, sour cream, tortilla corn chips and salsa.

ONE DISH CHICKEN POT PIE

Ingredients:

1 package refrigerated gluten-free pie crust dough (2 unbaked pie crusts)
2 cups cooked chicken, shredded
1 10.75-oz can gluten-free cream of chicken soup
1/3 cup cream
1/3 cup gluten-free chicken broth
Salt and pepper to taste
3/4 tsp poultry seasoning
2 potatoes, peeled and very thinly sliced
1-2 cups frozen mixed vegetables
1 4-oz can mushrooms
1/2 onion, finely chopped

Directions:

Preheat oven to 350°. Spray a large pie plate with non-stick cooking spray. Place one pie crust in the pie plate. Place the chicken in the bottom of the crust. In a small bowl, whisk together the soup, cream, chicken broth and seasonings; spoon the liquid over the chicken (it will be thick). Add the vegetables, making sure the sauce and vegetables are evenly distributed. Carefully lay the top crust on, crimping the edges. Put three slits in the top crust to allow steam to escape. Bake for 45-60 minutes or until vegetables are tender. If crust begins to get too brown, place foil around the edges of the crust to prevent burning.

CHINESE CHICKEN WINGS

Ingredients:
1 cup gluten-free soy sauce
1/2 cup orange juice
1/2 cup raspberry sherbet (most brands are gluten-free)
2 Tbsp brown sugar
1/4 cup canola oil
1 tsp ground ginger
1 tsp minced garlic
1 40-oz bag frozen chicken wing sections, thawed

Directions:
Stir together the first seven ingredients in a 9 x 13 inch pan, creating a marinade. Add the chicken wings to the marinade and cover for 30 minutes or overnight in the refrigerator. Turn the wings a few times to make sure they are marinating evenly. When ready to bake, preheat oven to 375°. Remove the cover from the dish and put in the oven, marinade and all. The marinade juices will bake down as the chicken cooks. Bake for 45 minutes or until browned, turning once.

BAKED CHICKEN FINGERS

Ingredients:
3 cups gluten-free corn flake cereal, crushed
1 cup toasted gluten-free oat bran
1 tsp seasoned salt
1 Tbsp dry minced onion
2 Tbsp olive oil
4 Chicken tenderloin pieces, rinsed and patted dry

Directions:
Preheat the oven to 350°. Spray a 9 x 13 inch pan with non-stick cooking spray. Pour the crushed cereal, oat bran, seasoned salt, and onion into the baking dish. Stir to combine. Pour the oil onto a small plate. Dip the chicken strips into the oil and then into the crumbs, pressing so that the coating sticks. Set each coated chicken strip to the side in the baking dish until they are all coated with the crumbs, then arrange in a single layer in the dish. If there is extra crumb mixture, that is fine. Bake the chicken fingers for 15-20 minutes or until the coating is turning golden brown and the chicken is cooked through. Note: For a spicier coating, add chili powder or Cajun seasoning to the cereal mixture.

A LITTLE BIT CHEESY CHICKEN BAKE

Ingredients:
1/2 cup cream
1/2 cup sour cream
1 10.75-oz can gluten-free cream of chicken soup
1/2 cup salsa
1/4 cup onion, chopped
6 gluten-free flour or corn tortillas, torn into small pieces
1-2 4-oz can green chiles, diced
1/2 cup Monterey Jack cheese, shredded
1/2 cup cheddar cheese, shredded
1 rotisserie chicken, deboned

Directions:
Preheat oven to 350°. Stir the first four ingredients together in a 9 x 13 inch baking dish. Add the remaining ingredients, stirring well. Bake for 30 minutes. Serve on a bed of cooked rice or gluten-free corn chips.

ONE PAN GREEK CHICKEN

Ingredients:
2 cups baby red potatoes, quartered
2 cups fresh green beans, trimmed
2 Tbsp olive oil
8 bone-in, skin-on chicken thighs
Salt free, gluten-free Greek seasoning

Directions:
Preheat oven to 400°. Spray a 9 x 13 inch pan with non-stick cooking spray. Place potatoes and green beans in a single layer in the prepared dish. Drizzle with olive oil. Top with chicken in a single layer. Sprinkle generously with Greek seasoning. Place in oven and bake until the chicken is completely cooked through, about 25-30 minutes. Broil for 2-3 minutes, or until golden brown and slightly charred. Serve immediately.

CHICKEN TAMALE CASSEROLE

Ingredients:
1/3 cup milk
1 egg
1 tsp ground cumin
1/8 tsp crushed red pepper flakes
1 cup cheddar cheese, shredded, divided
1 14.75-oz can gluten-free cream-style corn
1 8.5-oz box gluten-free corn muffin mix
1 4-oz can chopped green chiles, drained
1 10-oz can gluten-free red enchilada sauce
2 cups cooked chicken breast, cut into bite sized pieces
1/2 cup sour cream
Salsa

Directions:
Preheat oven to 400°. Spray a 9 x 13 inch pan with non-stick cooking spray. Whisk together the milk, egg, cumin and red pepper flakes in the baking dish. Add 1/2 cup of the shredded cheese along with the corn, dry corn muffin mix, and green chiles, stirring until moist. Bake for 15 minutes. Remove from oven and pierce entire surface liberally with a fork; pour the enchilada sauce over top. Top with the chicken and sprinkle with remaining 1/2 cup cheese. Return to the oven and bake for 15 minutes longer or until cheese melts. Remove from oven; let stand 5 minutes. Top each serving with a dollop of sour cream and a spoonful of salsa, if desired.

Note: Use a prepared rotisserie chicken to make this recipe extra easy and fast.

CHICKEN LUAU

Ingredients:
1/2 cup brown sugar
1/2 cup ketchup
1/4 cup gluten-free soy sauce
2 1/2 tsp minced ginger
1 1/2 tsp minced garlic
8 boneless, skinless chicken thighs
1 cup uncooked instant rice
1 15.25-oz can crushed pineapple, with juice
2 cups gluten-free chicken broth
1/2 cup honey

Directions:
In a small bowl, mix the first five ingredients in a re-sealable plastic bag. Add chicken and refrigerate for 8 hours or overnight. When ready to cook, preheat oven to 350°. Spray a 9 x 13 inch pan with non-stick spray. Put the rice into the prepare pan. Remove the chicken from the marinade and place on top of rice. Mix together the pineapple, chicken broth and honey and pour over chicken. Cover and bake for 20 minutes or unti chicken is cooked all the way through and rice is tender.

ITALIAN CHICKEN AND RICE

Ingredients:
2 cups prepared gluten-free spaghetti sauce
1 15-oz can Italian-seasoned diced tomatoes, undrained
1 cup long grain white rice, uncooked
1 1/2 lbs skinless, boneless chicken breast
1 tsp Italian seasoning
2 Tbsp fresh basil, chopped
1 cup mozzarella cheese, shredded
1/4 cup Parmesan cheese, grated

Directions:
Preheat oven to 375°. Stir the sauce, tomatoes and rice together in a 9 x 13 inch pan. Place the chicken breasts on top. Sprinkle the chicken with Italian seasoning and fresh basil. Cover the dish with a tight fitting lid or aluminum foil. Bake for 45 minutes or until the chicken is cooked through and the rice is soft. Remove the cover and sprinkle with the cheeses. Continue baking until the cheese has melted.

PEACHY PECAN CHICKEN

Ingredients:

4 skinless, boneless chicken breasts, halved horizontally into 8 thin cutlets
1 cup brown sugar, divided
1/2 cup pecans, chopped
4 fresh peaches, peeled, pitted, and sliced
1/8 tsp ground ginger
1/8 tsp ground cloves
1/2 cup gluten-free Russian dressing

Directions:

Preheat oven to 350°. Spray a 9 x 13 inch pan with non-stick cooking spray. Place the chicken in the prepared pan, and sprinkle with 1/2 cup of brown sugar and the pecans. Place peach slices over chicken, then sprinkle with remaining 1/2 cup brown sugar, ginger, cloves, and dressing. Bake for about 30 minutes, basting often with juices, until chicken is cooked through and juices run clear.

GLUTEN-FREE CHICKEN AND DUMPLINGS

Ingredients:
2 Tbsp butter
1 medium onion, diced
2 Tbsp gluten-free flour blend
1 3/4 cups gluten-free chicken broth
3/4 plus 1/2 cup milk
1 12-oz bag frozen mixed vegetables
2 cups cooked chicken, in bite sized pieces
1 tsp gluten-free seasoned salt
1/2 tsp thyme
3/4 cup gluten-free baking mix
1 egg
2 Tbsp butter, melted

Directions:
Pre-heat oven to 350°. Put butter and diced onion in a 9 x 13 inch baking dish and place in the oven to melt. When butter has melted, mix the gluten-free flour blend into the butter, stirring until completely blended. Pour in the chicken broth and then the 3/4 cup milk a little at a time, stirring until thickened and mixed well. Add the vegetables, chicken, salt and thyme. In a small bowl, stir together the remaining 1/2 cup milk, baking mix, egg and butter. Drop topping mixture by spoonful's over the chicken and vegetables. Bake 25-30 minutes or until toothpick inserted in center of dumplings comes out clean.

SWEET AND TANGY CHICKEN

Ingredients:
4 Chicken breast halves or tenderloin pieces
1 green bell pepper, sliced lengthwise
1/2 cup ketchup
1/4 cup water
1 can gluten-free condensed tomato soup
1/2 tsp apple cider vinegar
1 Tbsp prepared gluten-free Dijon mustard
1/3 cup packed brown sugar
3 Tbsp gluten-free dry onion soup mix

Directions:
Preheat oven to 350°. Spray an 8 x 8 inch baking dish with non-stick cooking spray. Lay the chicken pieces in the bottom of the pan and place the green pepper slices around the chicken. In a large bowl combine the remaining ingredients and pour over the chicken and green pepper. Bake for an hour or until chicken is cooked through. Serve over rice.

CHICKEN AND BROCCOLI WITH RICE

Ingredients:
1 can gluten-free condensed cream of chicken soup
1 cup gluten-free mayonnaise
1 tsp curry powder
1 cup water
1 6-oz package gluten-free seasoned wild rice mix
1 9-oz package frozen broccoli
1 cup cheddar cheese, shredded
4 boneless, skinless chicken breasts

Directions:
Preheat oven to 350°. Combine the soup, mayonnaise, curry powder, water, rice and seasoning packet, broccoli, and cheese in 3 quart casserole dish. Lay the chicken breasts on top. Cover and bake for 1 hour, or until chicken is cooked through.

CARIBBEAN CHICKEN AND RICE

Ingredients:
2 cups gluten-free instant white rice
2 cups gluten-free chicken broth
1 10.75-oz can gluten-free cream of chicken soup
1 10.75-oz can gluten-free cream of celery soup
4 Chicken breast halves or pieces
1 8-oz can pineapple rings
1/4 cup packed brown sugar
1/2 tsp nutmeg
1/2 cup orange juice
1/2 cup salted cashews, chopped

Directions:
Preheat oven to 350°. Spray an 8 x 8 inch baking dish with non-stick cooking spray. Spread the rice evenly in the bottom of the dish and pour the broth over the top. Stir in the soups until combined. Place the chicken pieces in the pan. Put the pineapple rings on top of the chicken pieces. Combine remaining ingredients and pour over the chicken and rice. Bake for an hour.

EASY LEMON GARLIC CHICKEN

Ingredients:
4 chicken breasts, cut in half
2-3 cloves of garlic, minced
4 Tbsp of olive oil
2 Tbsp fresh parsley, chopped
1/4 cup lemon juice
Salt and pepper, to taste

Directions:
Preheat oven to 350°. Spray an 8 x 8 inch baking dish with non-stick cooking spray. Place chicken in the pan and cover with remaining ingredients. Bake for 45-55 minutes, or until chicken is cooked through.

PEANUT BUTTER AND JELLY CHICKEN WINGS

Ingredients:
12 chicken wings, separated
2 Tbsp light olive oil
1 Tbsp gluten-free lite soy sauce
1/2 cup gluten-free peanut butter
3/4 cup gluten-free raspberry jelly
1 Tbsp brown sugar

Directions:
Preheat oven to 350°. Spray an 8 x 8 inch baking dish with non-stick cooking spray. Place chicken in the prepared pan. In a small bowl, whisk together the remaining ingredients. Pour sauce over the chicken, turning chicken pieces to coat evenly. Bake for 30-45 minutes, turning chicken wings once half-way through.

ONE PAN HONEY MUSTARD CHICKEN

Ingredients:
6 bacon slices
4 boneless skinless chicken breasts, pounded to 1/2 inch thickness
Seasoned salt (gluten-free)
1 jar gluten-free honey mustard salad dressing
1 cup fresh mushrooms, sliced (optional)
2 cups Colby or Monterey Jack cheese, or a mixture, shredded

Directions:
Preheat oven to 350°. In a large oven-proof skillet (such as cast iron), cook the bacon until crispy. Remove bacon from the pan and add the chicken and seasoned salt, and sauté in the bacon grease until browned on both sides. Spoon out and discard any left-over grease. With the chicken still in the pan, pour some honey mustard dressing over each piece of chicken, then layer with mushrooms, crumbled bacon, and shredded cheese. Put the skillet into the oven and bake 25-30 minutes, or until cheese is melted and chicken is no longer pink inside. Serve over buttered rice.

ROYAL CHICKEN

Ingredients:
2 large chicken breasts
1 onion, chopped
1 3-oz jar of capers, drained
3 garlic cloves, minced
1/2 cup fresh mint, chopped
1/2 cup fresh basil, chopped
1 4-oz jar anchovies, drained and chopped
1/2 tsp salt
1/4 tsp pepper
1 cup olive oil

Directions:
Preheat oven to 400°. Spray an 8 x 8 inch baking dish with non-stick cooking spray. Place the chicken in the prepared dish. Combine the remaining ingredients except the oil in a food processor and process until finely chopped. Then, with the machine on, pour the oil into the mixture and process until blended. Pour this sauce over the chicken, coating the pieces completely. Cover with a lid and bake until chicken is cooked through, but not over cooked, about 30-40 minutes.

SLOW COOKER HONEY SESAME CHICKEN

Ingredients:
4 large frozen chicken breasts
1/2 cup gluten-free soy sauce
3/4 cup honey
1 Tbsp olive oil
1 tsp onion powder
2 cloves garlic, minced
1 tsp salt
1/2 tsp pepper
1 Tbsp toasted sesame seeds

Directions:
Place all ingredients into a slow cooker. Stir until well combined. Cook on low for 3-4 hours, or until the chicken easily falls apart. Serve chicken over cooked quinoa or rice. Add extra sauce from the slow cooker on top if desired.

SWEET POTATO AND TURKEY HASH

Ingredients:
2 Tbsp extra-virgin olive oil
1 lb extra-lean ground turkey breakfast sausage
1/2 cup onions, diced
1/2 cup yellow pepper, diced
1 tsp garlic clove, minced
1 1/2 cup sweet potato, diced
Salt and pepper, to taste
1/2 cup shredded mozzarella cheese
1 egg per person, fried (optional)

Directions:
In a cast iron skillet, heat olive oil over medium high heat. Add ground turkey, onion, yellow bell peppers and garlic. Cook for about 10 minutes, stirring occasionally and add the sweet potato, salt and pepper. Cover the skillet and cook until tender, stirring occasionally. If necessary, add more olive oil or a little bit of water to cook the sweet potato.

While the sweet potato is cooking, pre-heat the oven to 400°. When the sweet potato is tender, spread the cheese on top and place the skillet in the oven. Remove from the oven when cheese has melted and serve immediately (add an egg on top of the hash, if desired).

DEEP DISH PAN PIZZA

Ingredients:
1 bag gluten-free pre-made pizza dough (refrigerator section)
1 14-oz jar gluten-free pizza sauce

Optional Toppings:
Sliced pepperoni
Italian seasoned turkey sausage, cooked and crumbled
Onions, chopped fine
Mushrooms, sliced
Black olives, sliced
Green bell pepper, diced
Mozzarella or blended Italian cheeses, shredded

Directions:
Preheat oven to 350°. Spray a 9 x 13 inch baking dish with cooking spray. Line the dish with the pizza crust dough, on the bottom and sides. Brush on a layer of pizza sauce. Add pepperoni and any other pizza toppings you would like. Top with shredded cheese and then repeat the layers, ending again with the shredded cheese. Bake for 20-30 minutes. Slice and serve.

GINGER HONEY GLAZED PORK CHOPS

Ingredients:
6 boneless pork chops
1/2 cup honey
1/4 cup brown sugar
1/4 cup apple cider vinegar
2 cloves garlic, minced
2 Tbsp gluten-free soy sauce
1/4 tsp ground ginger

Directions:
Preheat oven to 350°. Spray a 9 x 13 inch pan with non-stick cooking spray. Place the pork chops in the baking dish. Place remaining ingredients in a blender and combine to make a sauce. Pour the blended sauce over the pork. Bake for 40-45 minutes or until chops are cooked completely through. Serve over rice.

MAMA'S RAVIOLI BAKE

Ingredients:
1 lb Italian sausage, cooked and crumbled
1 25-oz package frozen gluten-free cheese ravioli
1 cup cottage cheese
1 28-oz jar gluten-free spaghetti sauce, divided
1 14.5-oz can diced tomatoes, drained
1 cup shredded mozzarella cheese
1 cup shredded Monterey Jack cheese
1 Tbsp grated Parmesan cheese

Directions:
Preheat oven to 350°. Spray a 9 x 13 inch pan with non-stick cooking spray. Reserve 1 cup of the spaghetti sauce in a small dish. In the pan, layer the ingredients in the following order: the cooked Italian sausage, ravioli, cottage cheese, spaghetti sauce and tomatoes. Top with the shredded mozzarella and Monterey Jack cheeses. Spread the reserved sauce over all. Cover with a tight fitting lid or aluminum foil. Bake for 30 minutes. Sprinkle Parmesan cheese over the top before serving.

QUICK AND EASY BREAKFAST CASSEROLE

Ingredients:
1 medium onion, peeled and diced
1 red bell pepper, diced
1 lb breakfast sausage, pre-cooked links or crumbled and browned
2 cups cheddar or mozzarella cheese, shredded and divided
1 20-oz bag frozen hash browns, thawed
6 eggs, whisked
1/3 cup milk
Salt and pepper to taste

Directions:
Preheat oven to 350°. Spray a 9 x 13 inch baking dish with non-stick cooking spray. Sprinkle the onion, and red pepper evenly in the bottom of the dish. Arrange the breakfast sausage in the dish, then spread 1 cup of cheese over the sausage. Add the hash browns and top with the remaining cheese. Pour the eggs and milk over all. Cover and bake for 20 minutes. Remove the cover and bake for an additional 10-15 minutes until the top begins to brown slightly. Remove and let rest for 5 minutes before serving.

PORK TENDERLOIN WITH ITALIAN ROASTED VEGETABLES

Ingredients:
1 cup zucchini, coarsely chopped
1 cup red onions, sliced
1 1/2 cup baby carrots
1-2 cups whole mushrooms
2-3 cups sweet potatoes, peeled and cut into chunks
1 apple, cored and chopped
1 pork tenderloin (1 lb), sliced into 8 pieces
1/4 cup olive oil
1 Tbsp balsamic vinegar
1/4 cup brown sugar

Directions:
Heat oven to 400°. Spray a 9 x 13 inch baking dish with non-stick cooking spray. Put vegetables, apple, and meat in the prepared dish. Drizzle with olive oil and vinegar and sprinkle with brown sugar. Bake 30-45 minutes or until meat is done and vegetables are tender.

PORK CHOPS AND POTATOES DINNER

Ingredients:
1 can gluten-free cream of celery soup
1/2 cup milk
1/2 cup sour cream
1 24-oz package frozen hash browns, thawed
1 cup cheddar cheese, shredded and divided
6 boneless pork chops
1 cup gluten-free French fried onion rings

Directions:
Preheat oven to 350°. Spray a 9 x 13 inch pan with non-stick cooking spray. In the dish, combine the soup, milk, and sour cream. Stir in the hash brown potatoes and 1/2 cup shredded cheese. Place the pork chops on top of the potatoes, top with remaining cheese and French fried onions. Bake for 50 minutes or until pork chops are cooked through.

HAM AND RICE CASSEROLE

Ingredients:
3 cups rice, cooked
2 cups ham, diced
1 28-oz jar of prepared gluten-free Alfredo sauce (or 2 cups of left-over homemade gluten-free Alfredo sauce)
1 bunch asparagus spears (14-18 spears), woody ends removed, spears cut into 1" pieces
1 cup sliced mushrooms, optional
Salt and pepper, to taste
2 cups crushed gluten-free almond crackers
6 Tbsp butter, melted

Directions:
Preheat oven to 350°. Spray a 9 x 13 inch baking dish with non-stick cooking spray. Combine the first five ingredients in the baking dish, add salt and pepper, and stir to blend evenly. Spread the cracker crumbs over the top and drizzle with the melted butter. Bake for 30 minutes or until hot and bubbly.

SLOW COOKER CRANBERRY PORK ROAST

Ingredients:
2.5 lb bone-in pork shoulder or pork-butt
1 15-oz can whole berry cranberry sauce
1/4 cup honey
1 package gluten-free dried onion soup mix

Directions:
Combine all ingredients in a slow cooker and cook on low for 6-8 hours or until pork shreds easily with a fork. Remove bones and shred meat.

MAPLE SPARERIBS

Ingredients:
2-3 lbs boneless country style spareribs
Garlic powder, to taste
1 Tbsp instant minced onion
3/4 cup maple syrup
1/4 cup gluten-free bottled French dressing
2 tsp apple cider vinegar
2 Tbsp gluten-free flour blend
1/4 cup cold water

Directions:
Trim excess fat from ribs and place in slow cooker. Sprinkle with garlic powder and onion. Mix syrup, dressing, and vinegar. Pour over ribs. At this point, the meat can marinate in the refrigerator, covered, for 1-2 hours or overnight. Cook on low 9-10 hours until meat is tender. Turn heat to high. Whisk flour into water; stir into juices in pot. Cover; cook 5-10 minutes until thickened.

Note: Marinating overnight tenderizes and adds flavor to the meat, but you can skip this step if desired.

FISH AND CHIPS

Ingredients:
4 cod or tilapia fillets (or other mild white fish)
3 eggs, beaten, in a medium size bowl
1/2 cup gluten-free all-purpose flour
1 1/2 cups gluten-free Japanese bread crumbs
Salt and pepper, to taste
1 12-oz package frozen French fried potatoes

Directions:
Preheat oven to 450°. Spray a 9 x 13 inch pan with non-stick cooking spray. Slice cod into strips and set in the bowl with beaten eggs. Put the flour and bread crumbs into the pan, mixing together with a fork. Place the fish pieces on top of the flour mixture. Turn the pieces to coat well. Sprinkle with salt and pepper. Place the potatoes in the same pan, around the fish. Bake 10-14 minutes or until fish is flaky and bread crumbs are golden brown.

SHRIMP AND RICE NOODLES

Ingredients:
1/2 lb package rice noodles, soaked in hot water per directions
2 Tbsp olive oil, divided
1 zucchini, sliced in quarter rounds
1/4 cup carrot, grated
Salt and pepper to taste
4 green onions, chopped and divided
1/2 cup low-sodium gluten-free tamari OR gluten-free
lite soy sauce
2 1/2 Tbsp brown sugar
1 1/2 Tbsp chili garlic sauce (more or less to taste)
1/2 lb frozen shrimp, thawed, rinsed and patted dry

Directions:
While preparing rice noodles per package directions, heat 1 Tbsp oil in the skillet then add zucchini and carrots, season with salt and pepper. Stir fry until just barely crisp-tender, 2 minutes. Add the green onions and stir fry for another minute. Add the (drained) rice noodles, the tamari or soy sauce, brown sugar and garlic sauce to the skillet. Stir fry for 1-2 minutes before adding the shrimp. Cook until the shrimp is pink and noodles are tender. Divide the noodle mixture between bowls, topping with reserved green onions.

BASIL PARMESAN CHICKEN SOUP

Ingredients:
4 cups gluten-free chicken stock
2 cups fresh spinach
2 cups cooked chicken, shredded
2 14-oz cans Great Northern or cannellini beans, rinsed and drained
1/3 cup gluten-free pesto
Parmesan cheese, grated

Directions:
Stir together chicken stock, spinach, chicken, and beans in a medium stock-pot. Bring to a boil and then reduce heat to simmering. Stir in the pesto and cook for an additional five minutes. Fill bowls with the hot soup and top with grated cheese. Serve alongside a loaf of crusty gluten-free French bread.

SAVORY VEGETABLE PIE

Ingredients:
2 cups broccoli florets, slightly cooked
1 7.5-oz jar marinated artichoke hearts, drained and sliced
1 cup zucchini, sliced very thin
1 4-oz can mushrooms
1/3 cup onion, chopped
1 cup cheddar cheese, shredded
1/2 cup gluten-free baking mix
1 cup milk
1/2 tsp salt
1/4 tsp pepper
2 eggs, beaten

Directions:
Heat oven to 400°. Spray a 9 inch pie plate with non-stick cooking spray. Stir together the broccoli, artichokes, zucchini, mushrooms, onion and cheese in pie plate. Add remaining ingredients and stir until blended. Bake 35-45 minutes or until golden brown and knife inserted in center comes out clean.

SWEET POTATO CRUNCH

Ingredients:

2 1/2 lbs sweet potatoes (4-6 potatoes), baked until very soft, skins removed
1/4 cup orange juice
1 tsp orange zest
1/4 cup sugar
2 eggs
1/2 cup (1 stick) butter, melted, divided
3/4 tsp baking powder
1 tsp vanilla extract
1/2 tsp + 1/8 tsp salt
1 cup chopped pecans (optional)
1/2 cup brown sugar

Directions:

Preheat oven to 350°. Spray a 9 x 13 inch baking dish with non-stick cooking spray. Place the sweet potatoes in the baking dish along with the orange juice, zest, sugar, eggs, 2 Tbsp butter, baking powder, vanilla and 1/2 tsp salt. Mash the sweet potatoes with a fork and stir mixture until well combined. Over the top sprinkle the pecans, brown sugar, 1/8 tsp salt, and remaining butter. Bake until bubbly, 40-45 minutes.

POTLUCK POTATOES

Ingredients:
1/4 cup (1/2 stick) butter
1 onion, chopped
1 16-oz container sour cream
1 cup small curd cottage cheese
1 10 1/2-oz can gluten-free cream of celery soup
1 8-oz package cheddar and Monterey Jack cheese, shredded
1 30-oz package frozen shredded hash brown potatoes, thawed
1 cup gluten-free corn flake cereal, crushed

Directions:
Preheat oven to 350°. Spray a 9 x 13 inch baking dish with non-stick cooking spray. In a small skillet, melt the butter over medium heat. Add onion, and sauté 3-4 minutes, or until tender. Put onion mixture and all other ingredients (except corn flakes) into the prepared baking dish. Stir until well blended. Top with crushed corn flake cereal. Bake for 45 minutes, or until hot and bubbly.

SPINACH AND RICE

2 Tbsp butter
1 10-oz box frozen spinach, thawed and excess liquid squeezed out
1/4 cup onion, chopped
1 1/2 cups water
1 cup instant rice, uncooked
1/3 cup cream or half and half
2 eggs, beaten
1 Tbsp gluten-free Worcestershire sauce
1 tsp salt
1/2 tsp black pepper
1 cup cheddar cheese, shredded
1 cup gluten-free butter crackers, crushed

Directions:
In a large skillet, melt the butter and add the spinach and onions, stirring over medium heat for a couple minutes. Add the water and rice, stir to combine. Stir in the cream, eggs, Worcestershire sauce, salt and pepper and cheese. Cover and cook for 15 minutes or until set. With 5 minutes left, sprinkle the 1/2 cup crushed crackers over the top, cover again and finish cooking.

APPLE CRANBERRY PAN BREAD

Ingredients:
10 soft gluten-free warm-n-serve dinner rolls,
cut into bite size pieces
1 10-oz can gluten-free cream of celery soup
3 eggs, beaten
1/4 cup butter, melted
1/2 tsp cinnamon
1/2 tsp salt
1/4 tsp pepper
2 cups gluten-free chicken broth
1 cup dried cranberries
1 onion, chopped fine
1 cup celery, chopped
2 tart green apples, peeled, cored and finely chopped

Directions:
Preheat oven to 350°. Place the cut up rolls in a single layer on a baking sheet and bake in the oven for 15 minutes until toasted. While the rolls are toasting, in a 9 x 13 inch pan, whisk together the soup, eggs, butter, cinnamon, and salt and pepper. Add the chicken broth, cranberries, onion, celery and apples. Stir in the toasted bread pieces until completely coated with liquid. Bake 45 minutes.

CORNY CORNBREAD

Ingredients:
1/2 cup (1 stick) butter
1 14.75-oz can gluten-free creamed corn
1 15-oz can whole kernel corn
2 tsp sugar
3 eggs, beaten
1 cup gluten-free sour cream
1 8.5-oz box gluten-free corn muffin mix
1 cup Monterey Jack cheese, shredded, divided

Directions:
Preheat oven to 350°. Place the butter in a 9 x 13 inch pan and place in the oven to melt. When butter has melted, remove the dish from the oven and stir in all the ingredients except 1/2 cup of the Monterey Jack cheese. Bake for 45-60 minutes. Spread the reserved cheese evenly on top and return to the oven until melted.

EASY GREEK SALAD

Ingredients:
4 cups romaine lettuce, torn into bite sized pieces
1 cup cherry tomatoes, cut in half
1 cup diced cucumber
1 red onion, sliced
1/2 cup black or Kalamata olives, pitted and drained
4-6 oz fresh mozzarella cheese, cubed
3/4 cup pepperoncini peppers, drained (optional)
1 rotisserie chicken, deboned (optional)
1 cup gluten-free Greek salad dressing

Directions:
In a large bowl, stir together and toss all the ingredients. Refrigerate for an hour or more before serving.

(This can easily be a main dish salad by adding the optional deboned chicken.)

OVERNIGHT BREAD PUDDING

Ingredients:
4 cups milk
1 cup cream
4 eggs, well beaten
1/3 cup sugar
1/3 cup brown sugar
1/2 tsp nutmeg
1/4 tsp cinnamon
1/2 cup raisins
6-10 gluten-free cake donuts (depends on size), broken into pieces

Directions:
In a slow cooker, whisk together the milk, cream, eggs, sugars and spices. Add the raisins and donut pieces to the pot, making sure that all the donuts are soaked with the milk mixture. Cover and cook on high for 4 hours, or on low 6-8 hours (or overnight).

ZUCCHINI OATMEAL DUMP CAKE

Ingredients:
1 1/2 cups shredded zucchini
1 cup old fashioned oats (check to make sure gluten-free)
1 1/2 cups applesauce
1 box gluten-free spice cake mix
1/2 cup brown sugar
1 cup (2 sticks) butter

Directions:
Preheat oven to 350°. Spray a 9 x 13 inch pan with non-stick cooking spray. Spread the zucchini in the bottom of the pan. Scatter the oatmeal evenly on top of the zucchini, and then spoon the applesauce on top of the oatmeal. Next, place the dry cake mix over the applesauce. Sprinkle the brown sugar over all. Slice the butter into pats and lay evenly on top. Bake for 40-50 minutes.

CLASSIC CHERRY DUMP CAKE

Ingredients:
1 30-oz can gluten-free cherry pie filling
1 box gluten-free yellow cake mix
1 cup (2 sticks) butter
Whipped cream or vanilla ice cream

Directions:
Preheat oven to 350°. Spray a 9 x 13 inch pan with non-stick cooking spray. Place the cherries in the pan. Spread the cake mix over the cherries. Slice butter and lay the pats evenly on the cake mix. Bake for 45-50 minutes, until cake is lightly golden brown. Serve with ice cream or whipped cream.

PEACHY GINGERBREAD DUMP CAKE

Ingredients:
3 15-oz cans sliced peaches, drained
1 box gluten-free gingerbread mix
1 cup (2 sticks) butter
Whipped cream or ice cream (or both)

Directions:
Preheat the oven to 350°. Spray a 9 x 13 inch pan with non-stick cooking spray. Place the peaches into the bottom of the pan. Cover the peaches with the dry gingerbread mix. Slice the butter into pats and lay on top of the dry cake mix. Bake for 40-45 minutes. Serve warm with whipped or ice cream.

BERRY'LICIOUS DESSERT CRISP

Ingredients:
1-1 1/2 cups each fresh or frozen strawberries, blackberries, blueberries, and raspberries
1 1/4 cup plus 1/2 cup granulated sugar
1 tsp cinnamon
1 cup gluten-free rolled oats
3/4 cup gluten-free flour blend
1/4 cup brown sugar, packed
1/2 tsp salt
1/2 cup butter, cut into 1/2-inch cubes

Directions:

Preheat the oven to 350°. Spray an 8 x 8-inch baking dish with non-stick cooking spray. Add the fruit to the prepared pan. Sprinkle the 1/2 cup granulated sugar over the fruit, stirring to coat. In a large bowl, combine the remaining ingredients, blending the butter in with a pastry cutter or two knives until it resembles coarse meal. Spread the topping evenly over the berries, then bake until the topping is golden brown, about 45 minutes. Serve warm with vanilla ice cream.

CHOCOLATE CHOCOLATE CHIP COOKIES

Ingredients:
1 18.25-oz package gluten-free chocolate cake mix
2 eggs
1 cup chocolate chips
1/2 cup vegetable oil

Directions:
Preheat oven to 350°. Mix together cake mix, eggs, chocolate chips, and oil in a large bowl. Make little balls with the dough and set on ungreased cookie sheets. Bake 4-10 minutes.

EASIEST EVER PECAN BARS

Ingredients:
3/4 cup white sugar
1/4 cup brown sugar
1/4 tsp salt
1 cup light corn syrup
1/2 cup (1 stick) butter, melted
3 eggs, beaten
1/4 tsp vanilla
1 cup chopped pecans
1 1/2 cups gluten-free shortbread cookies, crushed

Directions:
Preheat oven to 350°. Spray an 8 x 8 inch baking dish with non-stick cooking spray. Combine all ingredients in the baking dish except the cookies and mix well. Spread the crushed shortbread cookies evenly over the mixture and press down a bit into the pecan and sugar mixture. Bake for 45-50 minutes and let cool before serving.

CHOCOLATE SUNDAE CAKE

Ingredients:
2 cups gluten-free flour blend
1 1/2 cups white sugar
4 Tbsp cocoa
4 tsp gluten-free baking powder
1/2 tsp salt
1 cup milk
4 Tbsp butter, melted
2 tsp vanilla

Topping:
1 cup pecans, chopped
1 cup brown sugar
1 cup white sugar
4 Tbsp cocoa
2 cups cold water

Directions:
Preheat oven to 350°. Spray a 9 x 13 inch baking dish with non-stick cooking spray. In the bottom of the pan, use a fork to combine the flour, 1 1/2 cups white sugar, 4 Tbsp cocoa, baking powder, and salt. Add the milk, butter, and vanilla, whisking until smooth. Spread the chopped pecans evenly over the batter. Sprinkle the brown sugar, white sugar and cocoa over the pecans, using your fingers to make sure it is spread evenly and not in clumps. Pour the water over everything, but don't stir. Bake for 30-35 minutes. The surface of the cake should be pretty set but there is yummy, soupy chocolate underneath! Serve hot over vanilla ice cream.

PINEAPPLE UPSIDE-DOWN DUMP CAKE

Ingredients:
1 cup (2 sticks) butter
1 cup brown sugar
1 20-oz can pineapple slices
Red maraschino cherries, drained
1 package of yellow gluten-free cake mix

Directions:
Preheat oven to 350°. Spray a 9 x 13 inch pan with non-stick cooking spray. Place 1 stick of butter in the pan and place in the oven to melt. When the butter has melted, sprinkle the brown sugar evenly in the bottom of the pan. Arrange pineapple slices on the brown sugar and place a maraschino cherr in the center of each pineapple slice. Sprinkle the dry cake mi on top of the fruit and brown sugar. Slice the second stick of butter into pats and lay evenly on top of the cake mix. Bake for 40-45 minutes.

BUILD-YOUR-OWN LOADED BROWNIES

Ingredients:
4 large eggs
1 cup prepared chocolate-hazelnut spread, warmed until it is pourable
1/2 cup chopped hazelnuts
1/2 cup coconut
1/2 cup gluten-free granola (optional)
1/2 cup mini chocolate chips (optional)
Gluten-free caramel topping (for drizzling)
Confectioner's sugar

Directions:
Preheat oven to 350°. Spray an 8 × 8 inch pan with non-stick cooking spray. In a medium size mixing bowl, whisk the eggs until light and fluffy. Pour in the chocolate-hazelnut spread and continue whisking until well combined. Pour into the prepared pan. Spread the nuts, coconut, and any other toppings of your choice over the top of the batter. Bake for 25 minutes or until toothpick inserted in the center comes out clean. Let cool completely and then cut into squares and remove from pan. Drizzle each square with caramel and dust with confectioner's sugar, if desired.

GLUTEN-FREE PECAN PIE

Ingredients:
1/2 container gluten-free refrigerated pie and pastry dough
2/3 cup sugar
1/3 cup butter, melted
1 cup corn syrup
3 eggs
1 cup pecan halves or broken pecans
Sweetened whipped cream, if desired

Directions:
Heat oven to 375°. Using wax paper and a rolling pin, flatten prepared dough into a round crust large enough to fit inside pie plate. Press dough firmly against bottom and up side of plate. In a medium bowl, whisk together all ingredients exce pecans. Stir in pecans. Pour into crust-lined pie plate. Bake 40 to 50 minutes or until center is set. If edges brown too quickly, cover with a thin strip of foil. Cool before serving wi whipped cream.